How To Raise Comb Honey: Describing Improvements In Methods Resulting From Ten Years Practical Work, And Extensive Experiment

Oliver Foster

In the interest of creating a more extensive selection of rare historical book reprints, we have chosen to reproduce this title even though it may possibly have occasional imperfections such as missing and blurred pages, missing text, poor pictures, markings, dark backgrounds and other reproduction issues beyond our control. Because this work is culturally important, we have made it available as a part of our commitment to protecting, preserving and promoting the world's literature. Thank you for your understanding.

HOW TO RAISE
COMB HONEY.

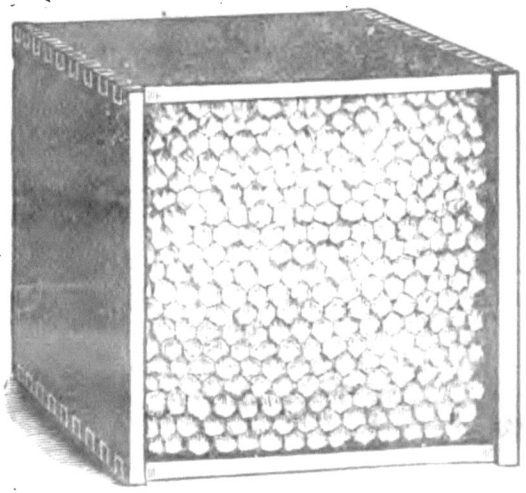

Describing Improvements in Methods Resulting from Ten Years Practical Work, and Extensive Experiment.

BY OLIVER FOSTER,
MT. VERNON, LINN COUNTY, IOWA.

Edson Fish, Printer, 1886.

How to Raise Comb Honey.

THIS delicious product of the bee-hive has always been classed among the choicest luxuries. As such, it has the advantage of being innocent and healthful.

Instead of impairing men's powers for usefulness, it tends to build them up. It is available, or should be, to all. Honey is not only a luxury—it is a staple article of food; and it is becoming such, more and more, as the science of producing it advances, and as prices correspondingly decrease.

With the same labor, and from the same bees, more honey can be produced in the extracted form than in the comb. Extracted honey is therefore cheaper, and it may be in better demand in some localities. But for beautiful comb honey, a decided preference is, and always will be shown.

It is useless to deny that, aside from its beautiful appearance, there is a rich flavor in ceiled comb honey that is not retained in the same honey after it is extracted. Perhaps it

"Wastes its sweetness on the desert air."

The granulation of extracted honey is also an objection with some. The reason why extracted honey granulates so much more than that in the comb, is that the texture of the former is disturbed by the agitation it receives while being thrown in a fine spray from the comb. The result is the formation of crystals at the approach of cold weather, and sometimes before.

But it is not our purpose to philosophize.

It is supposed that the reader is already interested in the management of bees for the production of comb honey, and that he is on the alert for the best and most practical "ways and means." If so, the first question for consideration is—

WHAT HIVE IS BEST?

We will not attempt a definite answer to this question. There is no doubt, however, that the hive that gives the most general satisfaction to-day, is the standard "Langstroth," in its variously modified forms, including what is known as the "Simplicity."

The more simple forms are decidedly preferable.

The style we use is more simple than the Simplicity. The size is 10 inches deep, 14¼ in. wide, and 18½ in long. They hold ten brood frames, of uniform size, having projecting top bars that rest in rabbits in the top edges of the end boards. We think this frame, as given us by Father Langstroth, has never been improved, and we doubt that it soon will be.

The hive should admit of a top story of the same size.

These hives possess nearly all of the advantages of all others, and there are a greater number of them in use than there are of any other kind—an item in their favor too great to be discussed here. We therefore recommend the L. hive for all purposes. (See "Invertible and Sectional Brood Chambers.")

Fig. 1.

LANGSTROTH HIVE WITH A SIMPLICITY UPPER STORY.

OUR IMPROVEMENT IN L. HIVES.

The beveled and shouldered joint between the upper and lower stories, and also between the hive and its cover, such as is found in the Simplicity and other hives, is considered an unnecessary protection against storms and wind by many of the most prominent apiarists, who have brought the experience of years to bear upon this question.

There are objections to these beveled edges, and the latest improved hives are square on the edges like a common box, as shown in the cut below.

Fig 2.

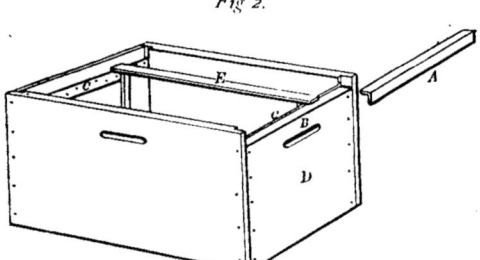

Our improvement consists of a rabbeted strip *A*, which is movable and fits into the back end of each hive body at *B*. It embraces the back ends of all the top bars, and thus holds the frames *E* down while the hive cover, honey board or top story, as the case may be, is pried loose. The pry being placed between the strip *A* and the part to be removed.

The back end board is ⅞ in. narrower than the sides and front. The front end is rabbeted in the usual way.

The frames rest on the edges of strips of No. 26 galvanized iron, *C, C*, which are 1x14¼ inches, and are nailed to the end boards, projecting ¼ inch above their upper inside edges.

The back end strip, *A*, as we call it, is ⅞x⅞x15 inches, with a rabbet, 9/16x9/16 inches taken from its lower inside corner. When it is in place over the frame ends at *B*, it closes the opening, leaving the top of the hive body level.

Bits of comb are always built in the space over the brood frames, and the lower frames often adhere to the upper parts, dropping loose, it may be, when half way out ; this device perfectly obviates these difficulties.

Having used upwards of 500 of these hives for four or five years, we could not be induced to discard the "back end stick."

Having the hive, we want a good strain of

BEES.

If you do not have them, get queens that have been bred for valuable qualities. They should be prolific. Their bees should be good honey gatherers, good winterers, and should have non-swarming tendencies. In our opinion, these qualities are more perfectly combined in the improved strains of Italians than they are in any other tested race.

SECTION BOXES.

It is almost unnecessary to say that all comb honey that is intended for table use should be stored in section boxes, containing but one comb each. There are many reasons for their use. We mention but one :

There is no sale for comb honey in any other shape in our important markets.

Sections holding about one pound of honey, bring from one to two cents more per pound than larger ones, and smaller ones are too tedious to handle for general use.

If they are 4¼ inches square and 1¾ inches wide, outside measure, they will weigh when filled about one pound, whether separators are used or not.

In using section boxes, we think some important points have been overlooked. Every available inducement should be used to inspire prompt, constant and energetic work in the boxes until they are finished.

In fact, we should *create a passion* for putting honey in boxes. This requires no magic. To accomplish it there should be no separation between the sections, and as little as possible between them and the brood.

There should be *free communication* between the sections in *every direction*. They should have deep slots on all 8 edges as shown in *Fig. 3*, so that bees can pass freely over the combs from end to end of the case, as well as from side to side, and from top to bottom.

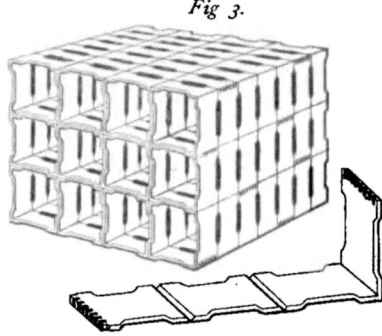

Fig 3.

You may not appreciate the importance of this until you have tried them.

When we take into consideration that the object on the part of the bees, in storing up honey in summer, is to have it accessible for winter consumption, and that in winter, the bees collect in a round ball, as nearly as possible, in a semi-torpid state with but little if any motion, except that gradual moving of bees from the center to the surface and from the surface to the center of this ball, we may imagine how unwelcome it is to them to be obliged to divide their stores between four separate apartments, each of which is four inches square and twelve inches long, with no communication between these apartments.

Another important object is secured by using open end sections.

Bees are much more apt to build the combs out solid to the end and bottom bars of the sections, if there is comb attached just the other side, with no bee space between, but with a wide opening through.

Honey will not ship safely, nor sell well, unless thus built out. Also, these openings on all sides, serve as a guide to insure straight combs.

Strenuous efforts are now being made to get all the honey stored in the sections and none in the brood nest. While we would not advise the practice of this with a view to feeding sugar for winter stores, still, it is an acquisition to be able to get a colony to put *all* their honey in the sections *while they are at it.*

Some unnatural operations are being resorted to, to *discourage* the deposit of honey in the brood chamber, such as contracting or inverting that apartment. While this plan has its advantages and may succeed, we would accomplish our object by milder means. If the foregoing and the following conditions are observed, bees will store their honey in the boxes, and not below. (See "Putting on Sections"; also, "How to Arrange the Sections in Cases.")

IMPROVEMENTS IN SECTION-BOXES.

We were probably the first to use these open-end sections. In March, 1884, we ordered a lot of them from B. Walker, of Capac, Michigan. He then listed them in his circular. In April, 1885, they were pictured and highly praised in the *Canadian Bee Journal*. We think they will become quite popular.

If the entrance slots are nearly ¼ inch deep, and only 3 inches long, tin separators will be no obstruction, and bees can pass between the outside row and the case.

The invention of the Section Box is probably next in importance to those of the movable frame and the honey extractor. They were first made of four pieces nailed together, as shown in Fig. 5. Next followed the "dove-tailed" section, (see cut on cover), but the greatest improvement was in making them all of one piece, bending them at three corners, (See Fig. 3.)

Several claim priority in this invention. It was original with the writer in 1877, when we gave to Ingham, Leslie & Co., of Michigan, a conditional order for a lot of them, to be made exactly as the Berlin company now make them—sliced, and with a V-shaped groove. These were not made, however, as expensive machinery would be required. We mention these points simply to show that we have tried to keep pace with the demands for improved appliances.

CASES TO HOLD SECTIONS ON THE HIVES.

As has been suggested under "section boxes," we want a case that will hold them in perfect contact with each other on all sides and ends, and when several tiers are used, one over the other, the bottoms of one tier should rest on the tops of the other. There should be perfect communication through the boxes in all directions, and between them and the brood chamber.

The case should admit of being filled and emptied quickly, without killing bees, without breaking or wrenching the boxes, and without jamming the combs; and at the same time, it should press and hold the sections so close together, from all sides, that no crevices will be left between them to be filled with propolis, by which the beauty of the sections would be marred.

On page 171 of *Gleanings in Bee Culture* for March, 1886, that able writer on bees, G. M. Doolittle, remarks as follows: "Propolis on sections is a nuisance, be the same little or much, and a plan which will allow of the filling of the sections with nice comb honey without changing the clean appearance which they present when placed upon the hive, will be heralded with delight by all, and give great honor to him who works out the plan."

These and other important advantages, the last mentioned one approximately at least, are combined in

THE "ADJUSTABLE" HONEY CASE."

We have had this case in use in our apiaries for two years past.

It has given such perfect satisfaction, and seems to so meet the demands of the day, that we have made arrangements to introduce it to the bee keeping public.

DESCRIPTION.

The case is made of four plane boards, B, B, C, C, (Fig. 4). They are cut $\frac{1}{16}$ in. narrower than the sections are high. A side and an end are nailed together in the form of a letter L. When two of these L shaped sections are placed together, they form the rectangular case, open at two opposite corners diagonally. The boards are mitred together at these open corners and are clasped together by the tin angle plates D. These corner plates are also bent L shape.

They are as high when folded as the sections, and $3\frac{1}{2}$ inches from the corner to each end. They have a small flange, bent outward on each end, E, and a double fold bent inward on each side, which forms sockets $\frac{3}{8}$ inch wide in which the ends of the boards slide in and out, thus expanding or contracting the case in length and width.

The folded side edges of the tin slide in saw grooves cut in the edges of the boards, as shown in the small figures, and the case is held rigid, whether open or closed. A small nail is driven through each of the slots I, into the wood, to prevent the case from opening farther than about ½ inch larger each way than when closed.

Foster's Adjustable Honey Case and Clamp.

Patented March 2, 1886.

Fig. 4.

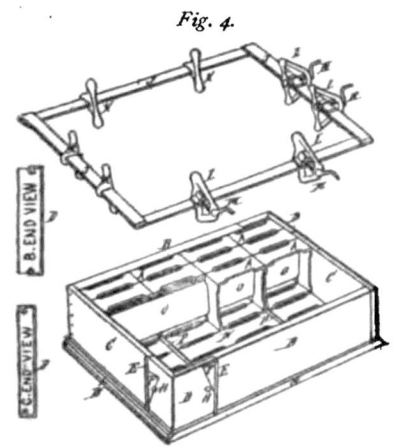

A, A, A, Section Boxes.
B, B, C, C, Plane side and end boards.
D, D, folded tin corner plates.
E, E, Flanges folded outward on ends of D.
F, F, Tin wedges which hold the case tight on the sections after clamping.
J, J, J, Iron clamp by which the case is drawn tight on the sections both ways.
H, H, Heads of nails through slots I.
O, O, O, Tin Separator, in place.
P, P, Narrow tin strips supporting separators.
N, N, N, Slotted honey board.

The case when closed is a little smaller than the tier of sections to be used.

To fill the case it is placed on a level board and opened out. The sections are then carelessly arranged inside, and then drawn into position by pressing the case together. A wrought iron clamp, J, is then slipped over the case, and by operating the screws M, the case is drawn so tight on the sections that all cracks between them are closed up, thus protecting the surface of the boxes from being soiled.

To prevent the spreading of the case when the clamp is removed, four simple tin wedges, F, F, are slipped under the flange, and the nail head.

This bottomless case of sections is then placed on the hive on a slotted honey board, which is level on top and has slots to correspond with those between the sections, save that the slots in the board are a little narrower, to secure perfect protection to the sections. If separators are used, they are simply dropped in between the rows of sections as each row is put in. (See O, Fig. 4.) They rest on the edges of two narrow strips of tin, P, P, that pass across each end of the case between the rows of sections at the bottom. These strips are movable, and securely held in place while handling, like the sections, by the lateral pressure of the case. The iron clamp is not a necessity, but it is very convenient where several colonies are kept. The case is equally adapted to use with or without separators. (See "Separators.") It can be used with or without an outer case. It can be "tiered up," "reversed," (inverted) or placed on end or on one side for "side storing."

COMB FOUNDATION.

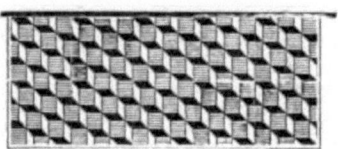

This may be considered a boon to bee-keepers, for use either in section boxes or in the brood frames, provided its use is not abused.

Any kind of foundation can be used in the latter, but, friends, if you do not wish to assist in damaging your markets for comb honey, our advice would be, use no foundation in section boxes heavier than about ten square feet to the pound; and that kind having "hair line" side walls, no heavier in the corners, is best. We have tried all kinds, and find that heavier foundation will sometimes show in the corners of the honey cells. While this does no harm to those who eat it, if it is noticed by the consumer—as it will be—it does harm to those who sell it.

HOW TO FASTEN FOUNDATION IN SECTIONS.

If you use only "starters," cut them ¼ inch shorter than the inside of section, and as wide as you wish; ½ inch will answer, but not so well as full sheets. These latter should be cut so that when fastened to the under side of the section top bar, they will just fill the box, save a space ¼ inch wide along the bottom, and a space at each end ¼ inch wide at the bottom and tapering to the corner at the top.

THE "PARKER" FOUNDATION FASTENER.

This will fasten these sheets quickly and securely in the sections. The cut shows how it is used. Lay the sheet on the top bar (inverted). Bring the top edge ⅛ inch beyond the center of the box. By operating the lever this ⅛ inch is pressed into the fibres of the wood.

Now bend the sheet up straight, and place the section right side up in

Fig. 5.

the case. Everything must be very warm, and the foundation and the sections must be dry.

We use a similar machine, worked by the foot, with an iron plate screwed to the under side of the pressing part. The wax is pressed by the rounded edge of this iron, which is kept warm by a lamp placed in the box to which the machine is fastened. A hole is bored through the box under the iron and over the lamp. Keep the iron just warm enough, and no lubricator is needed, and the foundation will be fastened more securely than in any other way.

HOW TO ARRANGE THE SECTIONS IN THE CASES.

Manage so as to have a supply of partly filled sections always on hand, at least some with comb partly built out.

To get these, remove the cases of honey before *all* the sections are entirely finished. Never market any, however, that are not perfectly finished and ceiled. Place one or two rows of these unfinished sections in every case you put on the hives.

Place a row of empty sections—with foundation—on each side of a row of unfinished ones; we mean "rows" of seven boxes each, across the case, not lengthwise. This stimulates immediate and energetic work in the cases. If you use

TIN SEPARATORS, (see fig. 4,)

the boxes may be arranged in almost any order, but if not, be careful or you will have "bulged combs." This rearrangement of boxes, however, enables us to arrest any bulging that may have begun.

HOW TO SECURE STRAIGHT COMBS WITHOUT SEPARATORS.

With the box and case herein described, this is not difficult. A bulged comb is one whose cells are built out too long on one or both sides. Of course the cells in the adjoining box will be correspondingly short.

To correct this, shave down all bulged sides with a honey knife to ⅛ inch below the edge of the section; also uncap all that is ceiled over too shallow. Now arrange the sections so that all full sides will be opposite full sides, and hollow sides opposite hollow sides. As the entrance slots between the sections are now just midway between the surfaces of the comb, there will probably be no further bulging. No arrangement is better adapted to use without separators.

Without the rearrangement described above, honey produced by the writer without separators, has brought the very highest market prices, and there was not one box in 500 but could be cased for shipment. Separators, however, are a great help in securing perfectly straight, even combs, every time. If only one separator is used near the middle of each case, it will do good service. You can use any number desired,

We should have our cases of sections all in readiness as far as possible, before the honey harvest begins.

PUTTING SECTION BOXES ON THE HIVES.
WHEN TO DO IT.

As a general rule, when the honey yield begins. At this time, in most localities, the brood chambers of all good colonies will be nearly full of brood, with but little honey. If not, it is sometimes advisable to take brood from weak colonies that are not in condition to work in sections, and give it to the strong. The weak colonies can then be built up and utilized for laying up winter stores for the strong, or in any other way, and the entire force of the strong colonies can be concentrated on the sections.

At the approach of the honey yield, place one case on each hive. When this case is about three-quarters full of honey, lift it and place an empty case under it. (See "How to Avoid Killing Bees.") When this one is nearly full place an empty one under it also.

You see the sections rest flat on the honey board, with no bee spaces, except under the board. In tiering up the cases, the upper tier of sections rests flat on the lower tier, and *fits it* by its own weight.

If all these conditions are observed, most good queens will keep the ten brood combs nearly full of brood throughout the honey flow.

The vacant comb, if any, will be mostly in the lower corners, and nearly empty. The honey will be in the sections.

But very few colonies will swarm. It is presumed that comb honey is our object, and not swarms.

HOW TO AVOID KILLING BEES
While Placing a Case Full of Them Over an Empty One.

It is a very easy matter. Rest the upper case in place on one end, while holding the other end up with one hand. Throw a few whiffs of smoke through between the cases. In a moment every bee will be up or down out of the way. Then clap down the upper case. If a few bees seem contrary, a thin strip of wood ⅛x1 inch, and 18 inches long, is handy with which to shove them back out of the way as the case is gradually lowered. We were surprised to find how quickly the case could be adjusted without killing bees.

CLOSED TOP SECTIONS.

These should have openings on all sides except the top. Some prefer to use these for the first case-full, even where tiering up is practiced. As this case is always on top, the bees are confined at the top until it is removed. Of course all sections that are added beneath must be open at the top. If no closed top sections are used, or if the top tier is removed before the others, the openings at the top are to be closed by means of a level board laid over them.

PROTECTION FROM PROPOLIS.

The tiers of sections should be pressed down, and made to fit close together. The clamp draws all the cases to exactly the same size. The slots between the sections will then all match, and the outside surfaces will thus be perfectly protected, provided the sections are accurately cut, and the cases and honey board are carefully adjusted.

TAKING OFF HONEY.

The upper case can be removed as soon as most of its sections are finished, or we can leave all on while the honey continues to come in from ore particular source, then take all off together.

The boxes should be nearly all finished before they are taken off. So don't add new cases unless you have reason to think they will be filled.

You can extract the honey from all unfinished sections of one crop. and then use them for the next crop and thus separate the different kinds of honey, and avoid carrying over much honey from year to year.

In removing the cases from the hive, apply the clamp and lift all together, or open the case and take out one box at a time, using a little smoke, and shaking and brushing off the bees. Nearly all of the bees can be shaken from a single case-full before opening it; but the neatest way to get them out is to place the cases in an empty hive a little to one side of the front of the hive from which they were taken. Fasten a wire cloth tube over the only opening at the entrance of this empty hive. Make the tube 6 inches long, ⅜ inch in diameter at the small end, and 1½ inch at the end attached to the hive. Place the hive in position so that the point of the tube will touch the front end of the hive containing the colony. In a few moments the bees will be marching "double quick" out through the tube, and in an hour or so every bee will be out.

SORTING AND CASING THE HONEY.

When the bees are all out, the honey should be taken to a bee-tight room or tent, where it can be sorted and cased for shipment or retail, without disturbance from robber bees. The windows should be covered with wire cloth. Each window should be provided with one or more wire cloth tubes, like those used to get bees out of cases. These should be near the top and pointing outward. In case of a tent, a large tube or two should point upward from the top. These are to enable all bees that may be carried in, to pass out readily without any attention from the operator.

Fig. 6.

SHIPPING CASES.

The cases for shipping and retailing honey, should be light, and glazed on one or both sides. Those holding but one tier are best. The sections should rest on narrow strips of wood ¼ inch thick, tacked to the bottom of the case over a sheet of manilla paper. This is to preserve the boxes from being daubed, in case the honey drips.

These cases should be in readiness before the honey is ready to be taken off.

The pleasures and profits in raising comb honey are realized by those who do everything at the right time and in the right way.

HOW TO REGULATE SWARMING.

When a colony is fairly at work in sections, the issue of a swarm greatly retards that work. While *all* swarming may not be prevented advantageously, all after swarms may be, and nearly all first swarms.

When a swarm issues, it may be managed according to what is known as the " Heddon Method," given us by Mr. James Heddon, of Dowagiac, Mich.

The object of this plan is to prevent all after swarming, and at the same time turn the working force of the old colony into the new.

It is, briefly, as follows :

The new swarm is hived on frames full of foundation, and placed on the old stand. The sections are taken from the old colony, part at a time, and placed on the new. The parent hive is moved a few inches to one side, and the entrance is turned around from the new one, for the first two days, until the new swarm "marks" their entrance. The old hive is then placed beside the new one, with their entrances facing the same way.

After about three days more, the old hive is gently moved to a new stand, while the bees are flying. Most of its bees then enter and unite with the new colony.

The old colony will be too weak to swarm, but, having a young queen and plenty of hatching brood, it will build up rapidly.

PERFORATED ZINC.

This has perforations, through which workers can pass, but not queens nor drones. The attention of bee-keepers was first called to this material by D. A. Jones, of Beeton, Ontario. Many are now experimenting with it with a view to utilizing it in controling natural swarming, and we look for some useful and practical developments in the near future. For the present, perforated zinc has an important place among the appliances for the production of comb honey.

If it is tacked to the under side of the slotted honey board, it prevents the passage of the queen into the section boxes.

If there is a scarcity of drone comb in the brood chamber, and room for it in the sections, the bees often invite her majesty "up stairs" for the sake of a little drone brood.

Such catastrophes rarely happen, however, where a full (ten L. frame) brood chamber is used, and where the sections are filled with worker foundation.

The zinc may be economized by cutting it into narrow strips and placing them between the slats of which the honey board is made. Shallow saw kerfs should be cut in the edges of the slats to receive it. While this idea was original with the writer, we find that it was also with others, and it has been recently published.

Appendix.

INVERTIBLE AND SECTIONAL BROOD CHAMBERS.

Many prominent bee-keepers are just now investigating the advantages of inverting the brood nest of colonies that are at work in sections.

There are three ways, in general, of doing this:

1st. By inverting the frames of comb separately.

2nd. By inverting the whole brood chamber or hive body, combs and all together.

3d. By having the brood chamber divided horizontally into shallow sections or tiers, and by transposing these parts, placing the lower one on top.

Each of these plans requires a different kind of hive and frame from the others.

THE OBJECTS OF INVERTING.

Nearly all of the first honey that is stored by a colony in the spring is placed just above the brood.

If there is no room over the brood, or, if that space is uninviting, as in case of improperly arranged sections, it is stored temporarily at the sides, until the upper brood hatches, when it is crowded into these vacated cells, thus gradually crowding the queen and her brood to the lower part of the combs, and widening the breech between them and the longed for surplus above.

The main object of inverting is to bring all this brood in the lower part of the brood chamber in close contact with the sections, thus stimulating work in them.

It will be observed that these same conditions would have existed when the first honey began to come in if the boxes had been in place, and if but little old honey had been present in the brood combs, excepting that no honey would have been below the brood.

When combs are inverted, the vacant space often left between the lower edge of the comb and the bottom bar of the frame is filled up solid with comb. This fact is of little or no importance, however, since all brood frames should be wired and filled with foundation from bottom to top, in which case no space will be left.

The experience of some seems to show that bees do not store honey as readily in inverted combs, since there is a little pitch to the cells.

As we have observed, the main object of inverting and transposing, is to bring the brood as close as possible to the surplus boxes.

It is obvious that none of these plans accomplishes this object perfectly, since the honey very often reaches from top to bottom of the brood chamber at the sides, while the brood does the same in the middle.

If we were to adopt this principle, we would divide the brood chamber into shallow but wide stories. Then, by *sorting the combs*, placing those containing most brood above, our object would be nearest accomplished, and there would be no need of inverting.

We would make these shallow hive bodies just like the bottomless ten frame L. hive body, excepting that they would be only about half as deep.

In order to get most of the brood where we want it, they should be at least ten frames wide.

Our L. combs can be easily changed into double the number of shallow ones. To do this, cut them in two horizontally, at the middle. Cut through comb, wood, wire and all. Now nail a top bar to the lower half, and a bottom bar to the upper half, and we have two complete frames full of comb.

If we want them "closed end," nail a cleat of tough wood to one edge of each end bar. The hives may be divided horizontally, also, and the extra depth made up by nailing cleats to the upper edge of the lower half. The division of the brood chamber horizontally into shallow sections for the purposes mentioned, is an important feature of a new hive recently patented by James Heddon, of Dowagiac, Michigan; and, while his patent does not cover the principle as we would apply it, we are indebted to him for the idea, as we are for many other valuable ones, and those wishing to test the principle should first consult the party named.

INVERTING SECTIONS.

This is done when they are nearly finished, that they may be filled out better at the bottom. The advantages of inverting sections have not been thoroughly tested, but no arrangement is better adapted to this practice than our Case herein described.

PATENTS.

We have had this Case and the Clamp patented, to enable us, by controling their manufacture and insuring good workmanship, to secure the mutual interests of all concerned.

All our other inventions and improvements herein or elsewhere described are freely given to the public, to make, use or sell.

Fraternally yours,
OLIVER FOSTER,
Mt. Vernon, Linn Co., Iowa.

A Card.

SHOULD the reader be in need of Bees, Queens, Bee-Hives, Section Boxes, Honey Cases, Comb Foundation, or other appliances for the Apiary, the writer of this pamphlet aims to keep these things always in stock. and would be pleased to mail, free, at any time, his latest Price-List, on receipt of name and address plainly writen on a postal card.

Address,

OLIVER FOSTER,
Mt. Vernon,
Linn County,
Iowa.

Price-List

— OF —

SUPPLIES FOR THE APIARY,

OFFERED BY

OLIVER FOSTER,

MT. VERNON, IOWA.

June, 1886.

The Adjustable Honey Case.

[*See Cut on next page.*]

I have had this case in practical use in my apiaries for two years past.

It has given such general satisfaction, and it has been so generally "called for" by those who have seen it, that I have decided to introduce it.

While it meets the long felt need of a case that will press and hold the sections compactly together on all sides, with no spaces nor partitions between them, it is cheap and simple, and it is easily and rapidly handled.

☞ A full description of the case and the best method of using it is given in **How to Raise Comb Honey**, a new pamphlet, full of useful information on improved methods resulting from years of practical work and extensive experiment. Price, 5 cents.

Foster's Adjustable Honey Case and Clamp.

PATENTED MARCH 2, 1886.

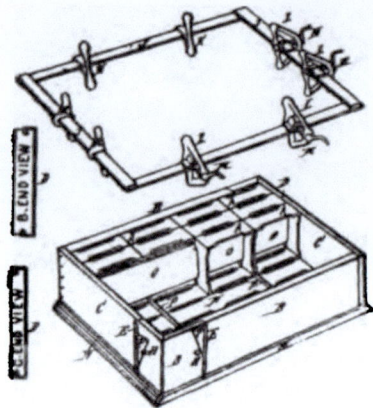

A, A, A, Section Boxes.
B, B, C, C, Plane side and end boards.
D, D, folded tin corner plates.
E, E, Flanges folded outward on ends of D.
F, F, Tin wedges which hold the case tight on the sections after clamping.
J, J, J, Iron clamp by which the case is drawn tight on the sections both ways.
H, H, Heads of nails through slots I.
O, O, O, Tin Separator, in place.
P, P, Narrow tin strips supporting separators.
N, N, N, Slotted honey board.

Bottomless, Invertible, Tiering.

The small Figures at the left show how the tin corners slide in the saw grooves.

PRICE-LIST.

THE ADJUSTABLE HONEY CASE.

Price.

Sample Case, put up complete, containing 28 Section Boxes, 4¼x4¼x1¾ in., one Slotted Honey Board, (See cut,) one Tin Separator and supporting strips................... 75
Wrought Iron clamp for same, best malleable iron fittings....$ 2 00
Only one clamp is needed in an apiary of any size.

The honey board just fits in the top of a Simplicity or L hive. It rests on the frames, and has a bee space under it. The top story goes over all, leaving a small space all around the case. These cases can be used on the "Heddon Hive," old or new style, and they can be made to fit any hive.

MATERIAL IN THE FLAT.

Adjustable Cases, including Tin Corners and Wedges, in crates of 5, 10, or 25, *Prices each—*

5 to 25...	18
30 to 50..	17
55 to 95..	16
100 or more..	15

SLOTTED HONEY BOARDS.

These are also in crates of 5, 10 or 25. *Price each* ....

5 to 25	15
30 to 50	14
55 to 95	13
100 or more	12

We think this is the most perfect honey board in the market. It has 32 slots, a little smaller than those between sections. It protects the whole bottom of the one-piece section, as plane slats in general use do not.

ONE-PIECE SECTION BOXES.

Size 4¼ x 4¼ x 1¾. They are about 7 to the foot after clamping. They are just right with or without separators. They have deep entrances on all sides, and are first-class.

100	65
500	$ 2 50
1,000	4 75
10,000	45 00

TIN SEPARATORS for the Adjustable Case, 2 cts. each.

These, when used, are simply dropped in between the rows of Sections.

SIMPLICITY HIVES. *In the flat.*

(*Hives and brood frames will be shipped from the factory at Davenport, Iowa; all other supplies from Mt. Vernon.*) They are well made, of good lumber. They are halved together at the corners. They are very strong, and easy to nail.

Two-Story Hives like the above, or same with a half-story cover— no insides—prices each—

1 to 16	95 cents.
16 to 20	91 "

20 to 50	90 "
50 to 100	85 "

Simplicity Hives, like the upper half of the above cut, consisting of one body and one cover—

2	such hives, in the flat	60 cents each.
4 to 10	" " "	58 "
10 to 20	" " "	55 "
20 to 50	" " "	51 "
50 to 100	" " "	48 "

Two of these make a two-story hive. One cover is then used for a bottom board.

BROOD FRAMES, for the above hives, drilled for wires; in the flat, per hundred.................................$1 50

No. 30 Tinned Wire for the above, 1-℔. spools, (enough for 175 frames), per ℔............................. 25

Folded Tin Bars for same, per hundred................. 35

SMOKERS—Clark's Cold Blast, 50 cents. By mail, 75 cents.

COMB FOUNDATION.

For Brood Combs, 6 square feet to the pound. Size, 8⅝x17⅛, in boxes of 5, 10, and 25 ℔s. each, 45 cts. per pound.

Very Thin Foundation for surplus honey, 10 to 12 square feet to the pound, size 3¼x15, in boxes of 2, 5 or 10 pounds each, per pound..................................... 60

☞ The quality of this Foundation is excelled nowhere. It is all papered. Samples by mail 2 cents.

BOOKS FOR BEE-KEEPERS.

Which I especially recommend.

BEE-KEEPER'S GUIDE, OR MANUAL OF THE APIARY..........$1 25
A, B, C, OF BEE-CULTURE, (paper)......................... 1 00
   do   do   do (cloth)........................... 1 25
HOW TO RAISE COMB HONEY, (pamphlet).................. 5

Mailed on receipt of price.

TERMS—My terms are cash with the order, and I guarantee satisfaction where such a thing is possible.

Address all orders to   **OLIVER FOSTER,**
                                    MT. VERNON,
                                          IOWA.

P. S.---ITALIAN BEES AND QUEENS BY THE POUND, NUCLEOUS, OR COLONY; SHIPPED SAFEFLY TO ANY PART OF THE UNITED STATES AND CANADA. BEES, 60 CENTS TO $1.00 PER LB. QUEENS, 30 CENTS TO $2.50. BROOD, 50 C. TO 80 C. PER L COMB PRICES VARY ACCORDING TO SEASON. COMPLETE PRICE-LIST FOR 1887, WILL BE READY IN JANUARY. THE SUPPLY FOR 1886 IS EXHAUSTED. SEND FOR ONE.

Yours Respectfully,

OLIVER FOSTER

DADANT'S FOUNDATION

is attested by hundreds of the most practical and disinterested bee-keepers to be the cleanest, brightest, quickest accepted by bees, least apt to sag, most regular in color, evenness and neatness of any that is made. It is kept for sale by Messrs.

THOS. G. NEWMAN & SON, Chicago, Ill.,
C. F. MUTH, Cincinnati, O.,
JAMES HEDDON, Dowagiac, Mich.,
F. L. DOUGHERTY, Indianapolis, Ind.,
CHAS. H. GREEN, Berlin, Wis.,
CHAS. HERTEL, Jr., Freeburg, Ill.,
E. L. ARMSTRONG, Jerseyville, Ill.,
ARTHUR TODD, Germantown, Philadelphia, Pa.
E. KRETCHER, Colburg, Iowa
ELBERT F. SMITH, Smyrna, N. Y.
EZRA BAER, Dixon, Lee Co., Ill.
CLARK JOHNSON, Covington, Ky.
C. A. GRAVES, Birmingham, Ohio.
M. J. DICKASON, Hiawatha, Kans.
ED. R. NEWCOMB, Pleasant Valley, N. Y.
J. W. PORTER, Charlottesville, Va.
J. B. MASON, & SON, Mechanic Falls, Maine.
J. A. HUMASON, Vienna, O.
Dr. G. L. TINKER, New Philadelphia, O.
D. A. FULLER, Cherry Valley, Ills.
J. M. SHUCK, Des Moines, Iowa.
ASPINWALL & TREADWELL, Barrytown, N. Y.
BARTON, FORSGARD & BARNES, Waco, Tex.

and numbers of other dealers. Write for SAMPLES FREE and Price-List of Supplies, accompanied with **150 COMPLIMENTARY** and **UNSOLICITED TESTIMONIALS** from as many bee-keepers in 1885. **We guarantee every inch of our Foundation equal to sample in every respect.**

CHAS. DADANT & SON,
HAMILTON, Hancock Co., ILL.

Friends, if you are in any way interested in

Bees or Honey

We will with pleasure send you a sample copy of the Semi-Monthly **Gleanings in Bee-Culture**, with a descriptive price-list of the latest improvements in Hives, Honey Extractors, Comb Foundation, Section Honey Boxes, all books and journals, and everything pertaining to Bee Culture. Nothing patented. Simply send your address, written plainly, to   A. I. ROOT, Medina, Ohio.
Mention this pamphet

A YEAR AMONG THE BEES,

BEING

A Talk about some of the Implements, Plans and Practices of a Bee-keeper of 25 years' Experience, who has for 8 years made the Production of Honey his Exclusive Business.

BY DR. C. C. MILLER.

Price 75 cents, by mail. This is a new work of about 140 pages, well-printed and nicely bound in cloth. Address,

THOS. G. NEWMAN & SON,
923 & 925 West Madison St.,   CHICAGO, ILL.

The American Apiculturist

will be

SENT FOUR YEARS

to any address, on receipt of $2.50. The above offer includes all the volumes of the Apiculturist from 1883 to Jan. 1, 1887. The first three volumes are

Handsomely Bound in Cloth,

and make splendid books for the library or centre table. If you want works that give the largest amount of valuable information on bee culture you should certainly order the above. The four volumes contain

Ten Hundred and Sixty Pages

of valuable reading matter, comprising articles from the pens of the most prominent writers and best apiarists in the world. All for the small sum of $2.50.

ADDRESS AMERICAN APICULTURIST,

WENHAM, MASS.

———TRIAL TRIP.———

THE CANADIAN BEE JOURNAL,

D. A. JONES, Editor.

FOUR MONTHS FOR 25 CENTS.

To all who mention having seen this advertisement in friend Foster's pamphlet, we will send our **BEE JOURNAL** for 25 cents for Four Months' trial trip. We make this offer believing that we only need to have subscriptions for a short time on our list to make them *permanent*.

20 PAGES   WEEKLY. $1 PER YEAR.

First weekly Bee Journal published in the world at $1 per annum.
Send for Sample Copies.

JONES, MACPHERSON & CO., BEETON, ONT., Canada.

BEE-KEEPERS' GUIDE OR MANUAL OF THE APAIRY, BY PROF. A. J. COOK:—It is elegantly illustrated, and fully up with the times or every subject that interests the bee-keeper. It is not only instructive, but interesting and thoroughly practical. It comprises a full delineation of the Anatomy and Physiology of bees. Price, $1.25.

Rays of Light.

A NEW PUBLICATION DEVOTED TO

BEE-KEEPING
AND
POULTRY-RAISING.

SUBSCRIPTION, - - 50 cts. per year

Sample Copy Free.

CHOICE ITALIAN BEES AND QUEENS.

Send for Catalogue.

Address all Communications to

J. J. MARTIN & CO.,
North Manchester, Indiana.

Bee-Keeper's Supplies.

STANDARD HIVES,

WHITE POPLAR SECTIONS,

AND

Bass-Wood Sections.

☞ IT WILL PAY YOU *BIG* TO WRITE FOR AN ESTIMATE BEFORE ORDERING ELSEWHERE.

The H. F. Moeller Mfg. Co.,

CORNER WESTERN AVE. & FIFTH ST.,
DAVENPORT, IOWA.

The Oldest Weekly Bee-Paper in the World.

ESTABLISHED IN 1861.

THE AMERICAN BEE JOURNAL,

Is the Recognized Leading Bee-Periodical in America.

ONE DOLLAR A YEAR, IN ADVANCE.
A Sample Copy Free, Upon Application.

The most successful and experienced bee-keepers in the World comprise its Corps of Contributors, and it is continually advancing progressive ideas upon the various topics of modern scientific Bee-Culture.

PUBLISHED BY

THOS. G. NEWMAN & SON,
923 & 925 West Madison St., CHICAGO, ILL.,

JOBBERS AND DEALERS IN

BEE-KEEPERS' SUPPLIES
INCLUDING

HIVES, SECTIONS,

HONEY & WAX EXTRACTORS, COMB FOUNDATION,

KEGS, PAILS, SEEDS, &c.

Illustrated Catalogue sent free upon application.

Printed by Libri Plureos GmbH in Hamburg, Germany